Conversions Useful in Fish Culture and Fishery Research and Managment

I0411354

Compiled by Brenda Rodgers Moore[1]
Andrew J. Mitchell

Fish Farming Experimental Station
U.S. Fish and Wildlife Service
Stuttgart, AK 72160-0860

[1]present address: 3008 Covewood Dr., Highpoint, NC 27260.

Leaflet 10
Washington, DC
1987
Revised January 2008

Contents

Abbreviations not defined in the lists of conversions.

atmosphere (atm)
avoirdupois (avdp)
British Imperial (B.I.)
Celsius (C)
day (d)
Fahrenheit (F)
hour (h)
international nautical
  mile (INM)
Kelvin (K)

mercury (Hg)
minute (min)
per (/)
percent (%)
per mille (%o)
Rankine (R)
second (s)
United States (U.S.; only
  with measurement)
water (H_2O)

Conversions

These tables of conversions from metric to English and English to metric measurements, as well as to metric and English from other systems such as British Imperial and troy, are primarily designed for use by fish farmers, fish culturists, and fishery technicians and scientists. The lists are compiled in the form we have found to be most useful. Also included are tables for conversion of Fahrenheit to Celsius temperatures, gallons to liters, and miles to kilometers.

acre (A) =	$4,046.9 \text{ m}^2$
	40.469 a
	0.405 ha
	$43,560 \text{ ft}^2$
	$4,840 \text{ yd}^2$
	160 rod^2
	0.00156 mi^2
	circle 235.4 ft diameter
	square 208.71 ft/side
acre-foot (A-ft) =	$1,233,500 \text{ L}$
	1233.5 m^3
	1.233 dam^3
	$1,233.500 \text{ kg H}_2\text{O}$
	$2,718,000 \text{ lb H}_2\text{O}$
	$325,850 \text{ gal}$
	$43,560 \text{ ft}^3$
	1 A of surface covered with 1 ft H_2O
ångström (Å) =	0.1 nm
	0.0000000001 m
	10^{-10} m
are (a) =	119.6 yd^2
	3.954 rod^2
	0.0247 A
	100 m^2
	1.00 dam^2
	100 ca
	0.01 ha
barrel, U.S. fruits and vegetables =	115.62 L
	13.12 pk
	3.28 bu
	30.55 gal
	$7,056 \text{ in}^3$
	4.083 ft^3

barrel, U.S. **liquid (bbL) =**	119.24 L 262.8 lb H_2O 26.23 gal_{BI} 31.5 gal 4.21 ft^3
barrel, U.S. **petroleum =**	158.98 L 34.97 gal_{BI} 42 gal
bushel, B.I. **(bu_{BI}) =**	36.368 L 0.036 m^3 9.607 gal 1.032 bu 2,219.36 in^3 1.284 ft^3 8 gal_{BI} 4 pk_{BI}
bushel, U.S. **(bu) =**	35.238 L 35,238 cm^3 64 pt, dry 32 qt, dry 4 pk 2,150.42 in^3 1.244 ft^3
centare *or* **centiare (ca) =**	1,549.9 in^2 10.764 ft^2 1.196 yd^2 1.0 m^2 0.01 a
centigram (cg) =	0.154 grain 0.000353 oz 3.53×10^{-4} oz 10 mg 0.01 g
centiliter (cL) =	0.338 fl oz 10 mL 0.01 L
centimeter (cm) =	0.394 in 0.0328 ft 0.0109 yd 10 mm 0.01 m

centimeter of mercury (cm Hg) =	0.444 ft H_2O
	0.193 lb/in^2
	27.74 lb/ft^2
	135.462 kg/m^2
	0.0132 atm
centimeter per second (cm/s) =	0.0328 ft/s
	1.969 ft/min
	0.000373 mi/min
	3.73 x 10^{-4} mi/min
	0.0224 mph
	0.6 m/min
	0.036 km/h
centner (zentner) =	50 kg
cubic centimeter (cm^3) =	0.0338 fl oz
	0.00211 pt
	0.00106 qt
	0.000264 gal
	2.64 x 10^{-4} gal
	0.061 in^3
	0.0000353 ft^3
	3.53 x 10^{-5} ft^3
	0.00000131 yd^3
	1.31 x 10^{-6} yd^3
	0.0353 oz H_2O
	1.0 g H_2O
	1.0 mL
	0.001 L
	1,000 mm^3
	0.000001 m^3
	10^{-6} m^3
cubic decimeter (dm^3) =	61.023 in^3
	0.0353 ft^3
	1,000 cm^3
	0.001 m^3
	1.0 L

cubic foot (ft³) =

28,317 mL
28,317 cm³
28.317 L
28.317 dm³
0.0283 m³
28,317 g H_2O
28,317 kg H_2O
957.5 fl oz
59.84 pt
29.92 qt
7.481 gal
1,728 in³
0.037 yd³
436,984 grain H_2O
998.85 oz H_2O
62.427 lb H_2O

cubic feet per minute (ft³/min) =

471.9 cm³/s
0.472 L/s
28.317 L/min
1,699 L/h
29.92 qt/min
1,795.32 qt/h
0.125 gal/s
7.481 gal/min
448.83 gal/h
10,772 gal/d
60 ft³/h
998.85 oz H_2O/min
62.427 lb H_2O/min

cubic feet per second (ft³/s) =

28.317 L/s
1,699 L/min
101,941 L/h
7.481 gal/s
448.83 gal/min
26,930 gal/h
60 ft³/min
3,600 ft³/h
646,400 gal/d

cubic inch (in³) =   16.387 g H_2O
16.387 mL
0.0164 L
16.387 cm³
0.00001639 m³
1.639×10^{-5} m³
0.554 fl oz
0.0346 pt
0.0173 qt
0.00433 gal
0.000579 ft³
5.79×10^{-4} ft³
0.00002143 yd³
2.143×10^{-5} yd³
0.578 oz H_2O
0.036 lb H_2O

cubic meter (m³) =   33,815 fl oz
2,113 pt
1,057 qt
264.2 gal
61,023 in³
35.31 ft³
1.308 yd³
2,204.6 lb H_2O
1,000,000 g H_2O
1,000,000 mL
1,000,000 cm³
1,000 dm³
1,000 L
1 st

cubic millimeter   0.001 mL
(mm³) =

cubic yard (yd³) =   764.559 L
764,600 cm³
0.7646 m³
0.7646 st
1,615.79 pt
807.89 qt
201.97 gal
46,656 in
27 ft³
1,685.5 lb H_2O

cubic yards per   12.743 L/s
minute (yd³/min) =   764.559 L/min
3.37 gal/s
201.97 gal/min
0.45 ft³/s
27 ft³/min

cup =
236.58 mL
236.58 cm^3
48 tsp
16 tbsp
8 fl oz
2 gi
8.344 oz H$_2$O

decare =
1,196 yd^2
0.2471 A
1,000 m^2
10 a
0.1 ha

deciare =
11.96 yd^2
10 m^2

decigram (dg) =
1.5432 grain
100 mg
10 cg
0.1 g

deciliter (dL) =
3.381 fl oz
0.211 pt
0.106 qt
6.103 in^3
100 mL
10 cL
0.1 L

decimeter (dm) =
3.937 in
0.328 ft
10 cm
0.1 m

decistere (dst) =
3.531 ft^3
0.1 m^3
0.1 st

dekagram (dag) =
0.353 oz
10 g

dekaliter (daL) =
2.642 gal
1.135 pk
0.284 bu
610.25 in^3
0.3531 ft^3
10 L

dekameter (dam) =	393.7 in
	32.808 ft
	1,000 cm
	10 m
dekastere (dast) =	353.1 ft^3
	13.08 yd^3
	10 m^3
	10 st
doppel zentner (dz) =	100 kg
	1.0 qL
	220.46 lb
dram, avdp (dr) =	1.771 g
	27.343 grain
	0.0625 oz
dram, fluid, B.I. (tL dr$_{BI}$) =	3.552 cm^3
	0.961 fl dr
	0.217 in^3
	60 minim$_{BI}$
dram, fluid, U.S. (fl dr) =	3.696 mL
	60 minim
	0.125 fl oz
	0.225 in^3
fathom (fath) =	1.829 m
	6 ft
	2 yd
foot (ft) =	304.8 mm
	30.480 cm
	0.305 m
	12 in
	0.333 yd
foot of water pressure =	304.79 kg/m^2
	0.434 lb/in^2
	62.427 lb/ft^2
	0.886 in Hg
	0.0295 atm
feet per minute (ft/min) =	0.5080 cm/s
	0.305 m/min
	18.29 m/h
	0.0183 km/h
	0.0167 ft/s
	0.0114 mph

feet per second **(ft/s) =**	30.48 cm/s 18.29 m/min 1.097 km/h 0.0114 mi/min 0.682 mph 0.593 kn
gallon, B.I. **(gal$_{BL}$) =**	4.545 L 4.803 qt 1.201 gal 277.420 in^3 0.161 ft^3 4 qt$_{BI}$
gallon, U.S. (gal) =	3,785.4 mL 3.785 L 3,785.4 cm^3 0.00379 m^3 3,785.4 g H$_2$O 3.785 kg H$_2$O 256 tbsp 128 fl oz 32 gi 8 pt 4 qt 0.833 gal$_{BI}$ 231 in^3 0.134 ft^3 0.00495 yd^3 58.416 grain H$_2$O 133.52 oz H$_2$O 8.345 lb H$_2$O
gallons per minute **(gal/min) =**	0.0631 L/s 3.875 L/min 5.45 t H$_2$O/d 6.009 ton short H$_2$O/d 0.134 ft^3/min 8.021 ft^3/h 0.00223 ft^3/ s 1,000 gal/min flow yields 1 A-ft in 5 h 26 min
gill, B.I. (gi$_{BI}$) =	142.066 cm^3 8.669 in^3 1.665 cup 1.201 gi 5 fl oz$_{BI}$

gill, U.S. (gi) =   118.291 mL
0.118 L
4 fl oz
0.25 pt
7.218 in^3
0.5 cup
8 tbsp

grain, avdp   64.8 mg
(grain) =   0.0648 g
0.0000648 kg
6.48 x 10^{-5} kg
1.0 grain tr
0.0417 dwt
0.0366 dr
0.00229 oz
0.00208 oz tr
0.000143 lb
1.43 x 10^{-4} lb

grain, troy   1.0 grain
(grain tr) =

grains per B.I.   14.26 ppm
gallon (grain/gal$_{BI}$) =

grains per U.S.   17.12 ppm
gallon (grain/gal) =   142.86 lb/1,000,000 gal

gram (g) =   15.432 grain
0.564 dr
0.0353 oz
0.0322 oz tr
0.0022 lb
0.0338 fl oz H$_2$O
0.0021 pt H$_2$O
1,000,000 μg
1,000 mg
10 dg
0.001 kg
1.0 mL H$_2$O
1.0 cm^3 H$_2$O
0.001 L H$_2$O

grams per liter   58.416 grain/gal
(g/L) =   0.134 oz/gal
0.999 oz/ft^3
8.345 lb/1,000 gal
0.0624 lb/ft^3
1,000 ppm
3.785 g/gal

hectare (ha) = 107,640 ft^2
2.471 A
10,000 m^2
10,000 ca
100 a
1.0 hm^2

hectogram (hg) = 3.527 oz
0.220 lb
100 g
10 dag
0.1 kg

hectoliter (hL) = 26.418 gal
3.531 ft^3
2.838 bu
100 L
10 daL
0.1 m^3

hectometer (hm) = 328 ft 1 in
109.36 yd
100 m
10 dam

**hundredweight,
long (cwt, long) =** 50.802 kg
0.0508 t
1,792 oz
112 lb
0.05 ton, long
1.12 cwt, short

**hundredweight,
short (cwt, short) =** 45.359 kg
0.0454 t
1,600 oz
100 lb
0.05 ton, short
0.893 cwt, long

inch (in) = 25,400 μm
25.40 mm
2.540 cm
0.0254 m
0.0833 ft
0.0278 yd

**inch of mercury
(in Hg) =** 344.07 kg/m^2
0.489 lb/in^2
70.45 lb/ft^2
1.129 ft H$_2$O
0.0334 atm

inch of water **(in H$_2$O) =**	25.40 kg/m^2 0.578 oz/in^2 0.0361 lb/in^2 5.201 lb/ft^2 0.0735 in Hg 0.00246 atm
kilogram (kg) =	15,432 grain 35,274 oz 2.2046 lb 0.0011 ton, short 1.057 qt H$_2$O 1,000,000 mg 1,000 g 10 hg 0.001 t 1.0 L H$_2$O
kilograms per **hectare (kg/ha) =**	0.892 lb/A
kiloliter (kL) =	264.17 gal 35.314 ft^3 1,000,000 mL 1,000 L 10 hL 1.0 m^3 2,204.6 lb H$_2$O 1,000 kg H$_2$O
kilometer (km) =	3,280.84 ft 1,093.61 yd 0.621 mi 0.540 INM 100,000 cm 1,000 m 10 hm 0.1 mym
knot (kn.) =	1.0 INM/h 1.15 mph
liter (L) =	202.9 tsp 67.6 tbsp 33.81 fl oz 4.23 cup 2.113 pt 1.057 qt 0.908 qt, dry 0.264 gal 35.27 oz H$_2$O 2.2046 lb H$_2$O

liter (L) continued =	61.025 in^3
	0.0353 ft^3
	0.00131 yd^3
	1,000 mL
	1,000 cm^3
	10 dL
	1.0 dm^3
	0.001 m^3
	1000 g H$_2$O
	1.0 kg H$_2$O
liters per minute (L/min) =	0.0044 gal/s
	0.264 gal/min
	15.852 gal/h
	0.0353 ft^3/min
	2.119 ft^3/h
meter (m) =	39.37 in
	3.281 ft
	1.094 yd
	0.199 rod
	1,000 mm
	100 cm
	10 dm
	0.001 km
	0.0001 mym
meters per minute (m/min) =	0.0547 ft/s
	3.281 ft/min
	0.0373 mph
	1.667 cm/s
	0.06 km/h
meters per second (m/s) =	3.281 ft/s
	196.86 ft/min
	0.0373 mi/min
	2.237 mph
	0.06 km/min
	3.60 km/h
microgram (µg) =	0.00001543 grain
	1.543 x 10^{-5} grain
	0.001 mg
	0.000001 g
	10^{-6} g
microliter (µL) =	0.001 mL
	0.000001 L
	10^{-6} L
	1.0 mm^3

micrometer (μm) =	0.00003937 in
	3.937×10^{-5} in
	1,000 nm
	0.001 mm
	0.000001 m
	10^{-6} m

mile (mi.) =	160,935 cm
	1,609.35 m
	1.609 km
	0.161 mym
	5,280 ft
	1,760 yd
	320 rod
	0.870 INM

miles per hour (mph) =	44.70 cm/s
	26.82 m/min
	1,609 km/h
	1,467 ft/s
	88 ft/min
	0.870 kn

miles per minute (mi/min) =	2,682.25 cm/s
	1.609 km/min
	96.561 km/h
	88 ft/s
	60 mph

milligram (mg) =	0.0154 grain
	1,000 μg
	0.001 g

milligrams per liter (mg/L) of water = 1 ppm (by weight)

milliliter (mL) =	0.203 tsp
	0.0338 fl oz
	0.002 pt
	0.001 qt
	0.061 in^3
	0.035 oz H_2O
	0.002 lb H_2O
	1,000 mm^3
	1.0 cm^3
	0.001 L
	1.0 g H_2O
	20 drops ($\pm$, depending on viscosity temperature, dropper bore, and force of propulsion)

millimeter (mm) =	0.0394 in
	1,000,000 nm
	1,000 μm
	0.1 cm
	0.001 m

million gallons	43.81 L/s
per day =	2,628.75 L/min
	11.57 gal/s
	694.44 gal/min
	41,667 gal/h
	1.547 ft^3/s
	92.83 ft^3/min
	5,569.67 ft^3/h
	133,700 ft^3/d

minim, B.I.	59.194 mm^3
(minim$_{BI}$) =	0.0592 cm^3
	0.961 minim
	0.00361 in^3
	0.0167 fl dr$_{BI}$

minim, U.S.	0.0616 mL
(minim) =	0.00376 in^3
	0.0167 fl dr

myriagram	22.046 lb
(myg) =	10,000 g
	10 kg

myrialiter	2,641.7 gal
(myL) =	353.14 ft^3
	283.78 bu
	83.86 bbL
	10,000 L

myriameter	6.214 mi.
(mym) =	10,000 m
	10 km

myriare =	247.1 A
	1,000,000 m^2
	100 ha

| **nanogram (ng) =** | 0.000000001 g |
| | 10^{-9} a |

nanometer (nm) =	0.000000001 m
	10^{-9} m
	10 Å

nautical mile (INM) =
1,852 m
1.852 km
6,076.115 ft
2,025.37 yd
1.151 mi

ounce, avdp (oz) =
28.3495 g
0.02835 kg
0.00002835 t
2.835×10^{-5} t
437.5 grain
16 dr
0.0625 lb
0.00003125 ton, short
3.125×10^{-5} ton, short
0.00002790 ton, long
2.790×10^{-5} ton, long
0.911 oz tr
0.959 fl oz H_2O

ounce, fluid, B.I. (fl oz$_{BI}$) =
28.416 cm^3
1.734 in^3
0.961 fl oz
8 fL dr$_{BI}$

ounce, fluid, U.S. (fl oz) =
29.573 g H_2O
29.573 mL
0.0296 L
29.573 cm^3
0.00002957 m^3
2.957×10^{-5} m^3
1.043 oz H_2O
0.0652 lb H_2O
8 fl dr
0.125 cup
0.0625 pt
0.0313 qt
0.00781 gal
6 tsp
2 tbsp
1.804 in^3
0.00104 ft^3

ounce, troy (oz tr) =
31.103 g
480 grain
17.555 dr
20 dwt
1.097 oz
0.0833 lb tr

parts per billion (ppb), by weight =	1.0 ng/mL H_2O
	1.0 μg/L H_2O
	3.785 μg/gal H_2O
	28.316 μg/ft^3 H_2O
	0.001 mg/L H_2O
	1.233 g/A-ft H_2O
	0.001 ppm (by weight)
	0.0000001 $\%$
	10^{-7} $\%$
	0.000001 $\%_{00}$
	10^{-6} $\%_{00}$

parts per hundred (pph), by weight =	1.0 g/100 mL H_2O
	10 g/1,000 mL H_2O
	10 g/L H_2O
	4.54 gL lb
	4.73 g/pt H_2O
	37.85 g/gal H_2O
	283.17 g/ft^3 H_2O
	10 mL/1,000 mL
	10 mL/L
	37.85 mL/gal
	10 cm^3/L
	37.85 cm^3/gal
	1.28 fl oz/gal
	1.34 oz/gal H_2O
	9.988 oz/ft^3 H_2O
	0.624 lb/ft^3 H_2O
	1.0 $\%$
	10 $\%_{00}$

parts per million (ppm), by weight =	1.0 μg/mL H_2O
	1.0 mg/L H_2O
	1.0 mg/kg
	3.785 mg/gal H_2O
	0.001 g/L H_2O
	0.00378 g/gal H_2O
	0.0283 g/ft^3 H_2O
	0.378 g/100 gal H_2O
	1.0 g/m^3 H_2O
	$1,233$ g/A-ft
	0.001 mL/L
	0.00378 mL/gal
	0.378 mL/100 gal
	1.0 mL/1,000,000 mL
	1.0 mL/1,000 L
	0.0584 grain/gal H_2O
	0.0702 grain/gal$_{BI}$ H_2O
	0.437 grain/ft^3 H_2O
	0.134 oz/1,000 gal H_2O
	0.999 oz/1,000 ft^3 H_2O
	1.0 lb/1,000,000 lb H_2O

parts per million (ppm), by weight, continued =	0.0000624 lb/ft^3 H_2O 6.24×10^{-5} lb/ft^3 H_2O 2.718 lb/A-ft H_2O 8.345 lb/10^6 gal H_2O 0.008 pt/1,000 gal 0.0599 pt/1,000 ft^3 1.303 qt/A-ft 0.326 gal/A-ft 0.0001 % 0.001 %$_{00}$
parts per thousand (ppt), by weight =	1.0 mg/mL H_2O 1.0 g/L H_2O 3.785 g/gal H_2O 28.316 g/ft^3 H_2O 15.432 grain/L H_2O 0.134 oz/gal H_2O 0.999 oz/ft^3 H_2O 0.1 % 1.0 %$_{00}$
parts per trillion (pptr), by weight =	1.0 pg/mL H_2O 1.0 ng/L H_2O 0.001 μg/L H_2O 0.000001 ppm (by weight) 10^{-6} ppm (by weight) 0.0000000001 % 10^{-10} % 0.000000001 %$_{00}$ 10^{-9} %$_{00}$
peck, B.I. (pk$_{BI}$) =	$9,092$ cm^3 0.00909 m^3 1.032 pk 554.84 in^3 0.321 ft^3 8 qt$_{BI}$ 2 gal$_{BI}$
peck, U.S. (pk) =	8.810 L 8 qt, dry 0.25 bu 537.605 in^3 0.311 ft^3
pennyweight, troy (dwt) =	1.555 g 24 grain 0.05 oz tr 0.00417 lb tr

picogram (pg) =   0.000000000001 g
10^{-12} g

pint, B.I. (pt$_{BI}$) =   568.26 cm^3
34.678 in^3
1.201 pt
1.032 pt, dry
4 gi$_{BI}$

pint, U.S. dry (pt, dry) =   550.6 cm^3
0.551 L
33.600 in^3
1.164 pt
0.582 qt
0.5 qt, dry

pint, U.S. liquid (pt) =   473.17 mL
473.17 cm^3
0.473 L
0.000473 m^3
4.73 x 10^{-4} m^3
473.17 g H_2O
32 tbsp
16 fl oz
4 gi
2 cup
0.859 pt dry
0.430 qt, dry
0.5000 qt
0.1250 gal
28.875 in^3
0.0167 ft^3
16.688 oz H_2O
1.043 lb H_2O

pound, avdp (lb) =   453.592 g
0.454 kg
0.000454 t
4.54 x 10^{-4} t
453.592 mL H_2O
453.592 cm^3 H_2O
0.454 L H_2O
7,000 grain
256 dr
16 oz
14.583 oz tr
1.215 lb tr
0.0005 ton, short
15.338 fl oz H_2O
0.959 pt H_2O
0.479 qt H_2O
0.120 gal H_2O
27.680 in^3 H_2O
0.0160 ft^3 H_2O

pound, troy (lb tr) =	373.241 g
	0.373 kg
	0.000373 t
	3.73×10^{-4} t
	5,760 grain
	240 dwt
	210.66 dr
	13.166 oz
	12 oz tr
	0.823 lb
	0.000411 ton, short
	4.11×10^{-4} ton, short
	0.000367 ton, long
	3.67×10^{-4} ton, long
pounds per acre (lb/A) =	1.121 kg/ha
pounds per million gallons of water =	0.120 ppm (by weight)
pound of water per minute =	0.4536 L/min
	0.120 gal/min
	0.0160 ft^3/min
quart, B.I. (qt_{BI}) =	1.136 L
	1.201 qt
	1.032 qt, dry
	69.355 in^3
	2 pt_{BI}
quart, U.S. dry (qt, dry) =	1,101 cm^3
	1.101 L
	2.328 pt
	2 pt, dry
	1.164 qt
	67.200 in^3
quart, U.S. liquid (qt) =	946.34 g H_2O
	946.34 mL
	0.946 L
	946.34 cm^3
	0.000946 m^3
	9.46×10^{-4} m^3
	64 tbsp
	32 fl oz
	8 gi
	4 cup
	2 pt
	0.859 qt, dry
	0.25 gal
	57.749 in^3
	0.0334 ft^3
	33.376 oz H_2O
	2.086 lb H_2O

quintal (qL) =   220.46 lb
100,000 g
100 kg
10 myg
1.0 dz

rod =   5.029 m
198 in
16.5 ft
5.50 yd

square centimeter   0.155 in^2
(cm^2) =   0.00108 ft^2
100 mm^2
0.0001 m^2

square decimeter   15.50 in^2
(dm^2) =   100 cm^2
0.01 m^2

square dekameter   119.6 yd^2
(dam^2) =   100 m^2

square foot (ft^2) =   929.03 cm^2
0.0929 m^2
144 in^2
0.111 yd^2
0.00002296 A
2.296 x 10^{-5} A
0.00000003587 mi^2
3.587 x 10^{-8} mi^2
square 12 in per side

square hectometer   107,600 ft^2
(hm^2) =   2.471 A
10,000 m^2
100 dam^2
100 a
1.0 ha

square inch (in^2) =   645.16 mm^2
6.452 cm^2
0.00694 ft^2
0.00077 yd^2

square kilometer   10,764,000 ft^2
(km^2) =   1,196,000 yd^2
247.1 A
0.386 mi^2
1,000,000 m^2
10,000 a
100 hm^2
100 ha

square meter (m²) = 1,550.007 in²
10.764 ft²
1.196 yd²
0.000247 A
2.47 x 10⁻⁴ A
0.0000003861 mi²
3.861 x 10⁻⁷ mi²
10,000 cm²
100 dm²
1.0 ca
0.01 a

square mile (mi²) = 2,590,000 m²
259 ha
2.590 km²
27,878,000 ft²
3,098,000 yd²
102,400 rod²
640 A

square millimeter 0.00155 in²
(mm²) = 0.01 cm²

square rod (rod²) = 25.29 m²
25.29 ca
0.253 a
272.25 ft²
30.25 yd²

square yard (yd²) = 8,361.3 cm²
0.836 m²
1,296 in²
9 ft²
0.000207 A
2.07 x 10⁻⁴ A
0.0000003228 mi²
3.228 x 10⁻⁷ mi²

stere (st) = 1.308 yd³
1.0 m³

stone = 6.350 kg
14 lb

tablespoon (tbsp) = 14.79 mL
14.79 cm³
3 tsp
0.50 fl oz

teaspoon (tsp) = 4.929 mL
4.929 cm³
0.333 tbsp
0.167 fl oz

ton, long =	1,016.05 kg
	1.016 t
	35,840 oz
	2,240 lb
	20 cwt, long
	1.120 ton, short
ton, metric (t) =	2,204.62 lb
	0.984 ton, long
	1.102 ton, short
	1,000 kg
	1,000 L H_2O
	10 qL
	10 dz
ton, short =	907.184 kg
	0.907 t
	32,000 oz
	29,167 oz tr
	2430.56 lb tr
	2,000 lb
	20 cwt, short
	0.893 ton, long
ton (short) of water per 24 h =	0.907 t/24 h
	37.80 L/h
	83.333 lb/h
	0.166 gal/min
	9.986 gal/h
	1.335 ft^3/h
yard (yd) =	91.44 cm
	0.914 m
	36 in
	3 ft
	0.182 rod
	0.000568 mi
	5.68 x 10^{-4} mi

Conversion Tables

Distance (miles and kilometers)

Miles to Kilometers

miles	km	miles	km	miles	km
1	1.61	10	16.09	100	160.94
2	3.22	20	32.19	150	241.40
3	4.83	30	48.28	200	321.87
4	6.44	40	64.37	300	482.80
5	8.05	50	80.47	400	643.74
6	9.66	60	96.56	500	804.67
7	11.27	70	112.65	600	965.61
8	12.87	80	128.75	700	1,126.54
9	14.48	90	114.84	800	1,287.48
				900	1,448.41
				1,000	1,609.35

Kilometers to Miles

km	miles	km	miles	km	miles
1	0.62	10	6.21	100	62.14
2	1.24	20	12.43	150	93.21
3	1.86	30	18.64	200	124.27
4	2.49	40	24.85	300	186.41
5	3.11	50	31.07	400	248.55
6	3.73	60	37.28	500	310.68
7	4.35	70	43.50	600	372.82
8	4.97	80	49.71	700	434.96
9	5.59	90	55.92	800	497.10
				900	559.23
				1,000	621.37

Capacity (Gallons and Liters)

Gallons to Liters

gallons	liters	gallons	liters
1	3.785	10	37.853
2	7.571	20	75.707
3	11.356	30	113.560
4	15.141	40	151.413
5	18.927	50	189.267
6	22.712	60	227.120
7	26.497	70	264.973
8	30.283	80	302.827
9	34.068	90	340.680
		100	378.533

Liters to Gallons

liters	gallons	liters	gallons
1	0.264	10	2.642
2	0.528	20	5.284
3	0.793	30	7.926
4	1.057	40	10.568
5	1.321	50	13.209
6	1.585	60	15.852
7	1.849	70	18.494
8	2.114	80	21.136
9	2.378	90	23.778
		100	26.417

Temperature[a]

Fahrenheit to Celsius

°F	°C	°F	°C
212.0	100.0	75.0	23.9
200.0	93.3	74.0	23.3
190.0	87.8	73.0	22.8
180.0	82.2	72.0	22.2
170.0	76.7	71.0	21.7
160.0	71.1	70.0	21.1
150.0	65.6	69.0	20.6
140.0	60.0	68.0	20.0
130.0	54.4	67.0	19.4
120.0	48.9	66.0	18.9
110.0	43.3	65.0	18.3
100.0	37.8	64.0	17.8
98.6	37.0	63.0	17.2
95.0	35.0	62.0	16.7
90.0	32.2	61.0	16.1
89.0	31.7	60.0	15.6
88.0	31.1	59.0	15.0
87.0	30.6	58.0	14.4
86.0	30.0	57.0	13.8
85.0	29.4	56.0	13.3
84.0	28.9	55.0	12.8
83.0	28.3	50.0	10.0
82.0	27.8	45.0	7.2
81.0	27.2	40.0	4.4
80.0	26.7	35.0	1.7
79.0	26.1	32.0	0
78.0	25.6	0.0	-17.8
77.0	25.0	-40.0	-40.0
76.0	24.4		

[a] Formula for conversion of temperatures:
$°F = (°C \times 9/5) + 32$
$°C = (°F - 32) \times 5/9$
$1.8 \, °C = °F - 32$
$°K = °C + 273$
$°R = °F = 460$

Celsius to Fahrenheit

°C	°F	°C	°F
100.0	212.0	50.0	122.0
99.0	210.2	49.0	120.2
98.0	204.8	48.0	118.4
97.0	206.6	47.0	116.6
96.0	204.8	46.0	114.8
95.0	203.0	45.0	113.0
94.0	201.2	44.0	111.2
93.0	199.4	43.0	109.4
92.0	197.6	42.0	107.6
91.0	195.8	41.0	105.8
90.0	194.0	40.0	104.0
89.0	192.2	39.0	102.2
88.0	190.4	38.0	100.4
87.0	188.6	37.0	98.6
86.0	186.8	36.0	96.8
85.0	185.0	35.0	95.0
84.0	183.2	34.0	93.2
83.0	181.4	33.0	91.4
82.0	179.6	32.0	89.6
81.0	177.8	31.0	87.8
80.0	176.0	30.0	86.0
79.0	174.2	29.0	84.2
78.0	172.4	28.0	82.4
77.0	170.6	27.0	80.6
76.0	168.8	26.0	78.8
75.0	167.0	25.0	77.0
74.0	165.2	24.0	75.2
73.0	163.4	23.0	73.4
72.0	161.6	22.0	71.6
71.0	159.8	21.0	69.8
70.0	158.0	20.0	68.0
69.0	156.2	19.0	66.2
68.0	154.4	18.0	64.4
67.0	152.6	17.0	62.6
66.0	150.8	16.0	60.8
65.0	149.0	15.0	59.0
64.0	147.2	14.0	57.2
63.0	145.4	13.0	55.4
62.0	143.6	12.0	53.6
61.0	141.8	11.0	51.8
60.0	140.0	10.0	50.0
59.0	138.2	9.0	48.2
58.0	136.4	8.0	46.4
57.0	134.6	7.0	44.6
56.0	132.8	6.0	42.8
55.0	131.0	5.0	41.0
54.0	129.2	4.0	39.2
53.0	127.4	3.0	37.4
52.0	125.6	2.0	35.6
51.0	123.8	1.0	33.8
		0.0	32.0

Bibliography

CBE Style Manual Committee. 1983. CBE style manual: a guide for authors, editors, and publishers in the biological sciences, 5th ed. Council of Biology Editors, Inc., Bethesda, MD

Cheremisinoff, N. P., and P. N. Cheremisinoff. 1980. Unit conversions and formulas manual. Ann Arbor Science Publishers, Inc., Ann Arbor, MI.

Herwig, N. 1979. Handbook of drugs and chemicals used in the treatment of fish diseases. Charles C. Thomas, Publisher, Springfield, IL.

Hoffman, G. L., and F. P. Meyer. 1974. Parasites of freshwater fishes. TFH Publications, Inc., Ltd., Neptune, NJ.

LeMaraic, A. L., and J. P. Ciaramella, editors. The complete metric system with the international system of units Abbey Books, Metric Media Book Publishers Somers, NY.

LeMaraic, A. L, and J. P. Ciaramella, editors. The metric encyclopedia. Abbey Books, Metric Media Book Publishers, Somers, NY.

U.S. Government Printing Office. 1984. Style manual U.S. Government Printing Office, Washington, DC.

Webster's New Collegiate Dictionary. 1960. G & C. Merriam Co., Springfield, MA.

Wellborn, T. L., Jr. 1974. Calculation of treatment levels for control of fish diseases and aquatic weeds. Mississippi State University, Ext Serv. Inf. Sheet 673.